How to Make a Great First Impression in North America

Kim Hunter

Cover illustration and design by Denis Lenzi

ISBN: 978-1-7324861-8-8

www.GreatFirstImpressionBooks.com

DEDICATION

For my students.

CONTENTS

Preface

As an English-language teacher from the United States, I have traveled to many countries.

In China, people asked me, "Where are you from? What do you do for a living? How much money do you make?" I was unprepared for the last question because in our country, people don't ask how much money you make when they first meet you.

In some countries, people kissed me on each cheek when they first met me. In India we put our hands together, bowed, and said, "Namaste."

Most people want to make a great first impression when they come to North America. I noticed that my foreign students, and people from other countries, would sometimes feel awkward when meeting for the first time. They sensed that our customs were different. It made me realize how truly important it is to understand and become fluent, not just with the language of a new country but also with its culture and customs. By doing so, it becomes easier to make a great first impression and a genuine connection with others.

Introduction

Welcome to North America! Whether you're here for school, a job, an interview, or just to explore, how do you make a great first impression? What does that entail, and how can you best present yourself?

Some people seem born confident. They know what to say and ask, their posture is straight, their smile is bright, and they look a person in the eye while giving a firm handshake. Maybe you have seen someone like that in real life or in the movies. The truth is they learned how to be that way, and so can you!

This book helps you make a great first impression and gives you a good start toward whatever you want to achieve in North America. It is also a guide for Americans who are just graduating and want to enhance their interview skills.

There are things in this world that are not in our control, but when it comes to making a first impression, you have control over many things: your attitude, appearance, eye contact, and attention, to name just a few.

It may be a cliché to ask how many chances you have to make a first impression, but, as former sales consultant Eliana Frank says, "First impressions are important because that is how people judge you. It's hard to change a first impression, and you may never get a second chance." Furthermore, first impressions are made quickly, so be prepared!

Chapter 1

It's All About
Your Energy!

*"At the end of the day people won't remember what you said
or did, they will remember how you made them feel."*
(Maya Angelou)

Have you ever noticed what makes a great teacher great? (Or a boring teacher boring?) It's their energy, their vitality! If they come across as being caring, enthusiastic, and passionate about what they are teaching, students can sense it. These are the same qualities you want to bring with you when you are meeting someone for the first time.

Gratitude and appreciation also project positive energy. "Nothing else so inspires and heartens people as words of appreciation," according to Dale Carnegie. If you think about it, just having an opportunity to make a great first impression IS a reason to feel grateful and appreciative!

Enthusiasm and Passion Earn You Extra Points

I once had a boss who said, "You can never be faulted for being passionate." One way to show your enthusiasm and passion is to prepare ahead for an interview or first meeting. You can research the company, school, or person you are meeting in advance. Having knowledge and being prepared will show your initiative and that you care.

If you don't have experience or a higher education, passion

and enthusiasm are a must! No one expects a young person, or someone changing roles, to have experience, but if they have enthusiasm and want to learn, that's invaluable!

A top hotel manager says he teaches his staff to have the attitude of: "The answer is YES! What is your question?" You can have the same enthusiasm in a job interview. If you are asked a question you don't know the answer to, say you don't know but you will find the answer and quickly get back to them.

Smile!

There's nothing like a million-dollar smile (or even a $10,000 smile!). A genuine smile is an essential part of the North American culture. How can you project a smile to someone you are meeting for the first time, even if you don't feel much like smiling? Use your imagination! Think of people who make you happy when you see them, or think of a comical situation that you are aware of to adjust your mood. Whether you are at a party or a job interview, the good feeling a smile creates is contagious.

Exception: If you meet someone and they are clearly upset, a big smile may not be appropriate. Be aware of the emotional climate so you can respond accordingly.

In general, a sincere smile with focused attention and appreciation toward the person you are meeting is a wonderful way to make a great first impression in North America.

Your Turn!

1. What are some things you can do to increase your positive energy?

2. Why is it important to smile?

Chapter 2

Be On Time

"You may delay, but time will not."
(Benjamin Franklin)

Don't ruin your first chance to make a good impression. Be on time! It seems obvious and yet when I interviewed candidates for a position at a company, it amazed me that several people showed up late, VERY late. I understand that unexpected things happen in life (that's life!), but at a minimum, the people who were running late should have contacted me to reset my expectations. That way I could have done other work, or I could have rescheduled their interview. Astonishingly, I found myself having to call *them* to find out if they were coming or not. None of these people got the job. After all, if they could be late for something as important as a job interview, how might they treat their future customers?

If you are always early, you'll never be late. It's a simple and useful phrase. It doesn't mean you should knock on the door 30 minutes early. Take advantage of any extra time to think about what you want to say, take a walk, or meditate (just don't fall asleep!). It's nice to have some breathing time before your first meeting. Being on time demonstrates professionalism and respect toward others.

Your Turn!

1. How do you feel when someone keeps you waiting?

2. If you have an appointment and you know you will be late, what do you do?

Chapter 3

You've Got to Care and Persevere

"From caring comes courage."
(Lao Tzu)

The best people in the service industry remember your name because they care. They may ask a detail about something you told them in the past. It's how they connect with and care for their customers.

A couple at a restaurant once told me they dine there every week just because they like the head waiter. He greets them by name, asks how they are, and if they want their "usual" meal. *He* is the reason they return. He connects with them, and that's the point! Caring communication allows us to connect with each other.

If you are trying to connect with someone, you must be present in the moment. Leave your phone and any other distractions aside! Even if you think the text message you are receiving might be important, when you are distracted it sends the wrong message to others in the room. It tells them they don't matter and *that* is not a good first impression!

Show interest in every person you meet. Make eye contact, shake hands, and follow what they are saying. Looking down or away when talking to someone in North America makes i seem that you are not interested in them.

Persevere

Not in a good mood? Had a bad day? It happens to everyone. As my favorite waiter puts it, "Bad attitude? Leave it outside!" Professionals don't whine and complain, they suit up, show up, and follow through. It doesn't matter what annoying thing is going on in their lives because "the show must go on," meaning you still have to do your job.

Even if you're not feeling 100%, act as if you are. Think about how you would like to come across, and behave that way. Think of things that make you smile, and you will feel better. Remember, postive energy is contagious.

It's also amazing how your mind can follow your body cues to change your mood. An old telephone sales trick is to bite a pencil before you talk. Doing this shapes your mouth into a semi-smile, sending a message to your brain that things are okay. People can "feel" your smile over the phone, and it really makes a difference.

Find what works for you to be more positive, and incorporate these things into your daily interactions.

Your Turn!

1. How can you show you care to someone you are meeting for the first time?

2. How can you maintain a positive attitude?

Chapter 4

Your Handshake Matters

And so does your body language

*"Dad trusted people based on their spirit
and their handshake"*

(John Carter Cash)

In some countries when you first meet, people come right up to you and kiss you on both cheeks. In other places they might nod slightly and look down. In North America, shaking hands is a professional and courteous way to greet someone new, and it is acceptable for men and women to shake each other's hands.

What makes a good or bad handshake? I have experienced too many wimpy handshakes. These are sometimes referred to as "dead-fish" handshakes because they feel like the other person's hand is a dead fish! A weak or limp handshake sends the wrong message; it may indicate a lack of interest or confidence. In contrast, when I receive a firm handshake that is equal to mine, I feel I'm meeting someone who is happy to meet me and is self-assured.

To begin a handshake, your right hand takes the other person's right hand, meeting in the juncture between the thumb and forefinger. The handshake is firm, but not too forceful, and after shaking hands up and down once or twice, you release. As you do this you introduce yourselves to one another. You can start by saying something like, "Hello, my name is Jane. Nice to meet you!" Or if the other person introduces themselves first you can reply by saying "Hi John, I'm Jane. Nice to meet you!" Remember to say the person's name in your reply, as it shows you listened and are interested in them. Speaking their name will also help you remember it.

How do you go from a good handshake to a great one? It involves having eye contact, a sincere smile, and positive energy. You can even imagine you are sending your good energy through your grip. All these things will show the other person you are really interested in them.

Common mistakes are:

- Looking down or away while shaking hands
- Barely shaking hands and then pulling away
- Tightening your right shoulder while shaking hands, making you seem nervous (and you might be!)
- Holding someone's hand too long — beyond 3 seconds (which can be awkward!)
- Jerking the other person's hand, instead of an even, flowing handshake that feels natural
- Gripping too tight (ouch!)

How do you improve? PRACTICE! Find a friend who is willing to work with you, and practice, practice, practice! It might seem strange at first, but better to make mistakes with a friend than with the person you want to impress. If possible, have a third person watch how you shake hands and give you feedback.

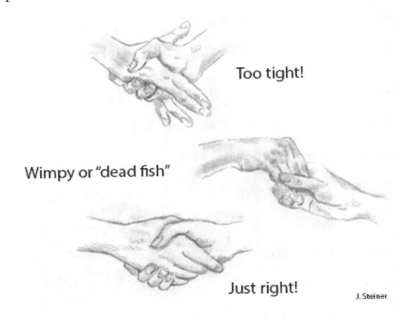

Too tight!

Wimpy or "dead fish"

Just right!

J. Steiner

What do you do if you have sweaty palms, sometimes referred to as "clammy hands"? Use a small amount of baby powder to instantly dry your hands. Applying antiperspirant to dry hands can prevent sweating. You may also want to carry a handkerchief or small cloth to dry your hands as needed.

Body Language

How we hold our bodies, our body language, is important because it conveys more than our words. Here are some

18

more suggestions to help you make a great first impression:

Have good posture! Hold yourself up straight when standing or sitting. If you are slouched or hunched over, you may appear to have low self-esteem, sorrow, or fear. Good posture conveys confidence.

Avoid tapping or fidgeting your hands, feet, or a pen, as it can indicate impatience or boredom, and many people find it annoying and distracting. If you are sitting down, sit back in your chair, and lean slightly toward the person you are with, as it shows interest in them.

When someone is speaking, keeping eye contact most of the time shows deep interest and is affirming and caring. Also, nodding your head in agreement with them occasionally while they speak shows you are listening. Of course, you must be sincere! If you don't agree with them and you are smiling and nodding your head, it may come across as being phony or an act.

Notice how close you stand to others. In general, North Americans like to have more personal space than other cultures. Standing too close can make them uncomfortable and want to back away. Also, standing too far away can feel awkward. A comfortable distance is to stand about an arm's length from someone you're meeting or speaking with.

After shaking hands, remember to keep your hands visible, either by your side if standing, or relaxed on your lap if sitting. Hands in your pockets or crossing your arms in front of you could send the message that you are defensive or not interested.

These are all things you can practice in front of a mirror or with a friend and notice the differences. You will also learn a lot by observing other people and how each person conveys something about themselves by the way they hold their bodies. Positive body language speaks volumes and helps make a great first impression!

Your Turn!

1. How do you develop a good handshake?

2. What kind of body language does a person have when they make a great first impression?

Chapter 5

Small Talk

"Talk is never just words."
(Bernard Beckett)

Casual conversation when meeting someone for the first time is called "small talk" because it is precisely that, talk that isn't very deep or meaningful. Yet making small talk is part of North American culture and being good at it can put others at ease, and make a great first impression.

Most relationships begin with small talk. If there are common interests and a good first connection, it can lead to more meaningful conversations later.

Beginning a conversation (or "breaking the ice") can be a challenge for a few reasons:

1. If you are not from this country, or even if you are from North America, strangers tend to be shy, and it can be intimidating to start a conversation with someone you don't know.

2. You have the additional challenge of what to talk about, and what NOT to talk about! That is because there are acceptable topics, as well as (taboo) ones to avoid.

3. North Americans are not comfortable with long silences, so having questions ready to ask can be a relief for

both parties. The good news is, once you get started, there's usually another question you can ask, based on their answer.

Here are some acceptable topics:

The weather – "It sure has been cold this week. Is that normal for this time of year?" or "The weather is lovely here. Is it like this most of the time?" The weather isn't the most interesting topic, but it's a common and safe conversation starter.

Where someone is from – "Where are you from?" When they answer, you can ask more questions, such as, "What part of the United States?" You might then ask them more about their hometown or where they live.

Family – People love to talk about their children, and in Western culture, they love their pets and consider them family as well. I've heard several Americans say something like, "I have a son, a daughter, and two cats" (or one dog, or whatever pets they have). Of course, you can ask all about their pets, which may in fact be one of their favorite topics!

Work – It is very common for North Americans to ask each other, "What do you do?" You can then follow up by asking about their work, such as what they like about it or how they became interested in it.

Entertainment – Books, film, television shows, and theater are all easy topics to ask about. "Do you enjoy reading?" "What TV shows are popular in your country now?"

Travel – "Have you seen much of the United States?" (Or Brazil, or wherever.) "What were some of your favorite places?" "Can you tell me more about that?"

Sports – Some people LOVE sports; others could not care less. So be sure to ask if they like sports before talking about how much you love basketball, baseball, or tennis. You could also ask: "What kind of sports do you like?" And if they answer: "None," continue with: "Really? What do you enjoy?" And carry on...

Food – Everyone eats, and lots of people have favorite foods they eat, or recipes they enjoy making. "What kinds of food do you like?" "What is your favorite local restaurant?"

Hobbies and interests – I enjoy finding out about people's hobbies and interests. If we have common interests, then we usually have a good conversation. If they like something I don't know anything about, it's an opportunity to learn, and sometimes it can be surprising. I met a man who made ships in bottles as a hobby, and each ship took one year to build!

Many people enjoy talking about themselves. Try to ask open-ended questions, such as, "Tell me about…" instead of questions that can be answered with "Yes," "No," or just a single word. This will give them an opportunity to tell you more about themselves.

Here are some *unacceptable* (taboo!) topics:

Religion – Religion is taken seriously by many people. The moral guidelines people live by are important and personal. To avoid any awkwardness, avoid the topic.

Politics – The United States is deeply divided when it comes to politics, and bringing up the subject puts you at risk of being on the "other" side. Meeting someone for the first time is not the time to begin a debate (or fight!) about politics!

Personal finance – When I visited China, people would ask me where I was from, what I did for a living, and how much money I made. I was surprised by the last question and unprepared to answer. In my culture, you don't ask how much money people make, certainly not at a first meeting! Money is personal to people in Western culture.

Sex – Mentioning this subject could be interpreted as harassment. Making suggestive or unwanted comments is entirely unacceptable.

Someone's weight – In some cultures, people just say it like they see it: "Wow, you look fat!" or "Look how skinny that person is!" In some places that could be a compliment, but in the United States it's an insult, so don't mention it!

Age – Yet another of those private matters. Though some people may come right out and tell you their age, most people won't, and they don't expect to be asked their age. However, it is appropriate to ask about the ages of someone's children.

Another way to make small talk easier is to remember the question words: who, what, when, where, how, and why.

For example, you could ask: "Who is your favorite author or actor?" "What are your hobbies?" "Where are you from?" "When did you move to New York?" "Why did you move here?" "How are your classes going?"

Small talk is a great thing to practice with a friend. You can take turns asking questions as well as responding to them. With practice, small talk will get easier and easier!

Your Turn!

1. Imagine you are meeting someone in the United States for the first time. What are possible questions you could ask?

2. What are possible questions they might ask, and how would you answer?

Chapter 6

Listen!

"If speaking is silver, then listening is gold."
(Turkish Proverb)

Listening sounds so easy, but it takes effort. When we listen to others, and respond in a way that shows we hear them, it gives validation to the speaker. Who doesn't want to be heard and validated? Giving someone attention (in a positive way) is one of the most precious gifts we can give. Therefore by being a good listener, we honor and respect them.

There are several ways to help someone feel you are really listening and interested in them. It is important to make eye contact. Unlike some cultures, in which eye contact is considered disrespectful, in North America, looking down or away makes it appear that you are neither listening nor interested. On the other hand, leaning forward and making eye contact shows that you are engaged in the conversation.

Another way is to nod and smile when appropriate. As you follow along, you can also say things such as "Yes," "Really?" "Huh." Strangely, when you show genuine interest in someone else, even if you have little to say, you seem interesting! I've seen this happen again and again. After the conversation, the person who did most of the talking thinks the other person is interesting and a good conversationalist.

If you don't understand what a person is saying, or if they are speaking too fast, you could say, "I'm sorry, I don't speak English well. Could you please repeat that?" or "Could you please speak more slowly?"

There's nothing wrong with asking a person to speak slower, or to repeat something you don't understand. Requesting this shows you care. And guess what? The speaker won't be bothered because they want you to understand too! Listening is more than just hearing the words. Genuinely paying attention allows you to get to know someone and understand what's most important to them.

Your Turn!

1. How do you let people know that you are listening to them?

2. How can you improve your listening skills?

Chapter 7

About ~~Mistaks~~ Mistakes

"Mistakes are proof you are trying."

(Anonymous)

Mistakes happen. We all make mistakes. Acknowledge your mistake right away and apologize if you need to, but don't be discouraged. Mistakes give us an opportunity to learn and even excel.

At the time you make a mistake it probably doesn't seem funny and it might even feel embarrassing. But in my classes, I expect students to make mistakes. Why? Because it means they are actively participating and making an effort. Consequently they learn from their mistakes and can experience the joy of accomplishment.

In North America, it is common to ask people how they are as part of greeting them: "Hello, how are you?" "Fine, and you?" "Fine, thank you." So, when I was in China, I would greet strangers in the same way in Mandarin: "Hello, how are you?" But I knew something was wrong when they didn't reply and I kept getting strange or confused looks. Then one day, one of my Chinese students pointed out that it isn't polite to ask strangers how they are. I could have felt badly, but actually I was relieved to learn my mistake and correct it so I could make a better first impression the next time.

How you manage mistakes can even lead to a positive outcome. My family once had dinner at a small restaurant, and the waiter made a mistake with our order. Then he kept us waiting after we asked him to correct it. Eventually, I told the manager who apologized and removed the item from our bill. He also offered us a free Sunday brunch the next time we came in. The free Sunday brunch we received later, celebrating a family member's birthday, was wonderful. More importantly, we kept going back to the restaurant, and I even wrote them a positive online review. Why? All because the manager handled the mistakes so well.

So remember, mistakes are a part of life. They help us learn and grow!

Your Turn!

1. How could you turn a mistake into a positive outcome?

2. What things can you do to prevent making mistakes?

Chapter 8

Personal Hygiene and Attire

"Good manners and bad breath will get you nowhere."
(Elvis Costello)

No one will tell you, "You stink!" Okay, maybe your mother will, but *don't* be stinky! (And that means your body and your breath.) If you think you can tell what you smell like, think again! I had a colleague who had bad breath. He had NO idea! I politely tried to offer him a mint, but he didn't get the hint (and take the mint). Like most people, I felt too embarrassed to tell him he had bad breath. As a result, I avoided sitting near him as much as possible.

Brush your teeth and tongue, and go the extra mile with a breath mint before you open your mouth to speak. No one will tell you your breath stinks, but the person who smells it will remember!

I like to chew a piece of gum to freshen my breath before I meet someone. I discard it before the meeting because chewing gum can be a distraction. It also makes it more difficult to understand the person speaking, especially if English is not their first language.

Pay attention to body odor (B.O.), especially if you are a smoker, as many people find smoking odors offensive. Bath and avoid strong-smelling perfume, aftershave, hair gel, and prays because these can be as offensive to some people as having body odor. There are unscented deodorants on the market if you need the extra protection.

Check your fingernails. Make sure they are clean and neat. If you paint your nails, make sure the polish is not chipped. Dirty and chipped fingernails are distracting and a sign of carelessness.

If you are going to a job interview, find out what people wear who are in similar jobs, and wear something just a little nicer. Make sure your shoes are clean, and shine them if needed. Don't wear a hat or excessive jewelry to a job interview. Keep it simple and avoid unnecessary distractions, including clothing that is too revealing. Ultimately, you want your physical appearance and hygiene to be a positive reflection of who you are.

Your Turn!

1. How should you prepare your attire and appearance for: School? A party? A job interview?

2. What are some ways you might improve your hygiene or appearance to make a great first impression?

Chapter 9

Lighten Up!

"Life is too important to be taken seriously."
(Oscar Wilde)

We've covered many tips in this book about how to make a great first impression. It may feel like a lot to remember, but try not to be stressed about it. Everyone is a beginner at some point in their lives. We learn best when we're having fun and enjoying the process.

When meeting someone for the first time, nothing makes a better first impression than being light and positive! If we are nervous and too serious it can make the other person feel uncomfortable. When we lighten up, it can create easy and memorable connections with others. Remember, the other person may be nervous too.

Be willing to see the humor in things and to laugh at yourself. For example, when I was traveling in Turkey someone spoke to me in Turkish, asking my name. I said, "Kim," and they replied "Sen!" (which means "You!" in Turkish), and again I said, "Kim," and again they replied "Sen!" We did this once more until we finally realized that "Kim" in Turkish means "who." I didn't realize that the conversation we were having was, "What is your name?" "Who?" "You!" "Who?" "You!". We laughed so hard and there was an instant connection. I will never forget that experience because it was so fun to laugh together at our funny miscommunication and at myself as "Mrs. Who."

Another time when I was worried and nervous about an upcoming event, I shared this with a friend and asked what I should do. After a long pause, he said jokingly, "You should worry as MUCH as possible, it will really help!" I immediately saw the humor and wisdom in that answer. Worrying is simply a waste of time, and it makes us feel bad.

What else can we do when we feel worried or nervous? Notice how your body feels when you have stress. Usually, we tense up in our shoulders or our bellies. Take a moment and see if you can sense that tension and then try to let it go, even if just a little. You can do this by relaxing and dropping your shoulders and softening your belly.

Some people also hold their breath when they are worried or nervous. It may sound obvious but don't forget to breathe and breathe deeply. Take a few seconds to notice your breathing, slow down, and relax with every exhale.

It's wonderful to lighten up and enjoy the moment whenever you can!

Your Turn!

1. What are some ways you can "lighten up" before meeting someone new?

2. Can you think of someone who made you feel good just by the way they greeted you?

Chapter 10

Follow up

"Silent gratitude isn't much use to anyone."
(G. B. Stern)

I have my own motto: "Suit up, show up, follow up!" Most people do the first two things on the list: they get dressed appropriately and show up for whatever opportunity they hope to find. But not enough people seem to understand that often the fortune is in the follow-up.

Following up can mean different things. For example, it could mean following through with a promise you made in a meeting, such as finding some information you were asked for and responding to the person or people in a timely manner.

Follow up can also mean sending a thank you note. Realizing that we live in the digital age, sending a thank you note via email is probably the right thing to do in most cases. If, however, you have the time and know the mailing address, there is nothing classier than sending an actual handwritten note via "snail mail" (through the post office). It doesn't need to be long or fancy, just something honest and positive. Use a nice note card, and *not* a piece of binder paper torn from a notebook.

Here is an example:

> *Dear ___,*
>
> *Thank you so much for taking the time to meet with me.* (Then a sentence on something you learned from or about them.) *I enjoyed your story about the first time you went to China.*
>
> (Conclusion) *I look forward to meeting you again. (OR, I hope to hear from you soon.)*
>
> *Sincerely,*
>
> (Your first and last name here)

Look over your note several times, checking for spelling and grammar. If English isn't your first language, then keep it simple! Read or show it to a friend or teacher if you have any concern about it. Just remember to send it!

At this point, your "job" of meeting them is over. How they respond, whether you get the position, or whether you are accepted into the school is no longer in your hands. It may be a good time to review what you did well, and what you would like to improve. But try to avoid repeatedly telling yourself, "I should have done (this or that)." You not only hurt yourself, but you miss a basic truth: simply by showing up and making an effort, you have set yourself up for success. That's why it's so important to really look at what you did right, and practice the things you want to improve.

Challenge yourself to meet new people and be confident that you can make a great first impression!

Your Turn!

1. You meet a few people at a party that you enjoyed talking to, or you want to thank the host or hostess for inviting you. What can you do?

2. After a job interview what might you write to follow up?

Conclusion

The world is an ever-smaller place with many people, cultures, and customs. We have more opportunities than ever to connect with each other and to express our unique qualities. When we reach out to connect for the first time, we want people to know we are trustworthy, kind, confident, and prepared. Great first impressions can open doors of opportunity. Whether it's making new friends, being accepted into a school, or getting a new job, the world needs your unique talents and positive energy more than ever!

Acknowledgments

I wish to thank my students whose desire to learn inspired me and helped me to write this book.

I would also like to thank the following people for their help and inspiration: Victoria, Bern, Philip, Jordan, Michel, Abby, Tess, Karl, Natalie, Ceilia, Gary, Ela, Denise, Jeanelle, Eliana, Mel, Viviane, Wynn, Beth, Janelle, Deborah K., Lulu, Deborah T., Robert, Patty, Lynn, Amy, Lucy, Ms. Pizzo, Melanie, Elise, Sean, and my loving husband Larry.

Made in the
USA
Monee, IL